YOUR KNOWLEDGE HAS VALUE

Kim H. Bui

Democracy in Greece, 1974 – 2009

Democracy in Greece, 1974 – 2009: Comparing the Database of Political Institutions and Freedom House

GRIN Verlag

Bibliografische Information der Deutschen Nationalbibliothek:

Die Deutsche Bibliothek verzeichnet diese Publikation in der Deutschen National-
bibliografie; detaillierte bibliografische Daten sind im Internet über http://dnb.d-
nb.de/ abrufbar.

Imprint:

Copyright © 2009 GRIN Verlag GmbH
Druck und Bindung: Books on Demand GmbH, Norderstedt Germany
ISBN: 978-3-656-34196-3

This book at GRIN:

http://www.grin.com/en/e-book/207046/democracy-in-greece-1974-2009

GRIN - Your knowledge has value

Der GRIN Verlag publiziert seit 1998 wissenschaftliche Arbeiten von Studenten, Hochschullehrern und anderen Akademikern als eBook und gedrucktes Buch. Die Verlagswebsite www.grin.com ist die ideale Plattform zur Veröffentlichung von Hausarbeiten, Abschlussarbeiten, wissenschaftlichen Aufsätzen, Dissertationen und Fachbüchern.

Visit us on the internet:

http://www.grin.com/

http://www.facebook.com/grincom

http://www.twitter.com/grin_com

Jacobs University Bremen

Measuring Democracy in Greece, 1974 – 2009

Comparing the Database of Political Institutions and Freedom House

Kim Bui

Mailbox 078

Comparing Political Systems

Due Date: November 16, 2009

Word Count: 1643 words

Introduction

This paper seeks to determine whether Greece has been a democratic country in the period of 1974 – 2009 using two measures of democracy—the Freedom House and the Database of Political Institutions. A brief introduction of the two measures will first be given, followed by the categorization of Greece according to each measure. Finally, the paper will discuss merits and demerits of each measurement to come to the conclusion regarding which type of regime Greece possesses and which measure is more accurate.

Two Measures of Democracy: Freedom House and the Database of Political Institutions (DPI)

Freedom House

Freedom House attempts to assess the democratic freedom of 193 countries and 15 related and disputed territories in the world on an annual basis (Freedom House 2009c). It aims at reflecting both non-governmental and governmental actions that result in the real world of rights and freedoms, by examining the two broad evaluation categories—political rights and civil liberties on a seven-point scale ranging from 1 to 7 (with 1 representing the highest level of freedom and 7 the lowest level of freedom). Each country is categorized based on the average of the individual scores on political rights and civil liberties, as "Free" (average score of 1.0 – 2.5), "Partly Free" (average score of 3.5 – 5.0) or "Not Free" (average score of 5.5 – 7.0). Upward and downward trend arrows are also assigned to indicate positive and negative trends which are not significant enough to alter ratings (Puddington 2008).

The DPI

The Database of Political Institutions (DPI) is a cross-country empirical database focusing on 177 countries' political and institutional characteristics, as well as their variation over time (Beck et al., 2001). It seeks to determine democracy by election outcomes in multi-party elections based on the 7-level-scale Executive Indices of Political Competitiveness (one for presidential and one for parliamentary elections; comprising of Legislature and Executive Index of Electoral Competitiveness—see table 2, 3—appendix); at least a level of 6 is required for the designation as democracy (Keefer et al. 2006). According to the DPI, a unanimous victory (100 percent of seats) of one party in multi-party elections is equivalent with unfree and unfair elections, and consequently, undemocratic regimes. By the same token, a single party winning 75 percent of seats implies a suspicious election, but not necessarily an undemocratic regime (Bogaards 2007).

Measuring Democracy in Greece

Freedom House Measures

During the period between 1974 and 2009, Greece has been categorized as "Free" with an average score of approximately 1.79 by Freedom House (see figure 1 and table 1 (appendix)). From 1974 to 1979, Greece maintained the score of 2 in both political rights and civil liberties. Political rights experienced improvement in 1980 (from the score of 2 to 1), leading to the improved of the average score to 1.5. The positive trend ceased in November 1984, when Greek political rights fell back to 2, and this score preserved until the end of 1989. Since 1990, Greece has achieved advance in political rights, scoring 1 in 19 successive years (1990 – 2008). As for civil liberties, Greece was stable in 1974 – 1992 with the score of 2. However, 9 years from 1993 to 2001 witnessed a slight contraction in civil liberties when the score dropped to 3. Despite the diminishing civil liberties, Greece still earned the designation of "Free" with 2 as the average score. In 2002, civil conditions improved and have stabilized ever since with the score of 2, resulting in the rising average score from 2 to 1.5. However, there was a downward tendency in Greek overall freedom in December 2008 (denoted by a downward arrow in Freedom House Survey data (Puddington 2008)), though the incident was not significant enough to set back the ratings. Regarding electoral system, since November 1988, Greece's parliamentary system has been appreciated as free and fair by Freedom House, rewarding in Greece classified as an electoral democracy (Freedom House, 2009b).

Figure 1: Freedom House's scores of Greece, Period 1974 – 2008

(Freedom House, 2009b)

The DPI Measures

In 1974, Greece carried out its first free multi-party election after decades of military regime ruling the country since 1967 with the participation of 81.5 percent of population. Election outcomes marked the victory of New Democratic Party with 54.37 percent of votes (Inter-Parliamentary Union 2009). Compared with the DPI's Indices of Electoral Competitiveness, for the 1974 election, Greece achieved level 7, and thus, qualified as a democracy. During 1975 – 2006, Greece was categorized by the DPI as democratic with a level value of 7 (World Bank 2009). The 2007 and 2009 election witnessed the victory of New Democratic and Panhellenic Socialist Movement (PASOK) with 41.84 percent and 36.64 percent of votes respectively (Inter-Parliamentary Union 2009). Again, Greece maintains in level 7 of electoral competitiveness and is a democracy based on the DPI's scale. Therefore, in 1974 – 2009, Greece is a democracy according to the DPI.

Merits and Demerits of Freedom House & the DPI with Respect to Greece

According to both Freedom House and the DPI measurements, Greece is categorized as democracy in the period of 1974 – 2009. Although achieving identical conclusion, the two measurements express specific merits and demerits in their distinctive methodologies, requiring further discussion.

The DPI

The DPI with its disaggregated, simplified and objective data proves to be a time- and effort-saving tool of measuring democracy. Unfortunately, as a result, the DPI lacks the comprehensiveness expected of a democracy measurement. It's hardly capable of showing up- or downward democratic tendencies. It's unable to demonstrate underlying political, socio-economic forces behind these democratic movements. With the 7-level-scale Indices of Electoral Competitiveness, the DPI better qualifies as a classifier instead of a measure. In case of Greece, no further conclusion apart from Greece—a democracy can be reached. This is a disappointing result considering the data Freedom House offers.

The DPI's principals of determining democracy in light of elections and election outcomes are susceptible to plausibility. Plausibility primarily comes from its adoption of multi-party elections as an indicator of democracy. Indeed, multi-party elections are a very representative manifesto of democracy as they originate from, and thus present political competition—an indispensible democracy ingredient. Its mere presence, however, is far from sufficient for democracy. A closer look at the two indexes of electoral competitiveness also discloses a fundamental flaw of the DPI. It disregards elections with absolute victory as free and fair. It suspects overwhelming victory and questions the existence of democracy. By these thresholds, the DPI fails to capture the very basis of elections: election victory mirrors the support of electoral majority (Bogaards 2007). As for Greece, these weaknesses seem to suffer from less severity. The explanation lies in Greece's multi-party system, which favors the presence of many parties with no one approaching 50 percent of votes and seats (Caramani 2008).

Another problem of the DPI comes from its data's outdating tendency. Democracy requires frequent updates while the availability of its determinant, according to the DPI—election is subject to office term, which is apparently not on an annual basis (four years, in case of Greece). Time discrepancy disables the DPI's capability of reflecting democratic fluctuation, consequently reduces its accuracy and reliability. The most recent illustration for this is the Greek 2008 riots which exerted considerable pressure to Greek democracy (and is recorded as a negative democratic trend by Freedom House) but exploded in time between elections, thus was out of the DPI's reach.

Freedom House

While the DPI stresses data flow's objectivity and simplicity, Freedom House pioneers in the opposite direction with its highly comprehensive and subjective statistics. Thanks to the exhaustive data, the state of democracy is reflected thoroughly with its two broad indicators—political rights and civil liberties. Freedom House also tests electoral system to define the electoral democracy, giving a more specific picture of democracy. As for Greece, in the period of 1974 – 2009, it has been categorized as a democratic country. If it's all that the DPI can conclude, Freedom House makes a further step when assess and determine the state of political rights and civil liberties. For a country with relatively stable democracy like Greece, Freedom House democracy measure is a better preference for its highly detailed indicators.

Conclusion

After the careful examination of Freedom House and the DPI democracy measurements, two conclusions can be extracted: Greece is a democracy during 1974 – 2009, and Freedom House democracy measure possesses superiority in comparison with the DPI. The fact that Greece has been a democracy is recognized by both measures; however, Freedom House succeeds in providing a more detailed and accurate picture when it takes into account political rights, civil liberties and electoral democracy status. As for the DPI, its measure shows several weaknesses mainly stemming from its principals of taking election outcomes as democracy indicators. In conclusion, with respect to Greece, Freedom House is the better choice for democracy measurement.

Appendix

Table 1: Freedom House scores of Greece, Period 1974 – 2008

Year	Political Rights	Civil Liberties	Average Score	Status
1974	2	2	2	F
1975	2	2	2	F
1976	2	2	2	F
1977	2	2	2	F
1978	2	2	2	F
1979	2	2	2	F
1980	1	2	1.5	F
01/1981 - 08/1982	1	2	1.5	F
08/1982 - 11/1983	1	2	1.5	F
11/1983 - 11/1984	1	2	1.5	F
11/1984 - 11/1985	2	2	2	F
11/1985 - 11/1986	2	2	2	F
11/1986 - 11/1987	2	2	2	F
11/1987 - 11/1988 *	2	2	2	F
11/1988 - 12/1989 *	2	2	2	F
1990 *	1	2	1.5	F
1991 *	1	2	1.5	F
1992 *	1	2	1.5	F
1993 *	1	3	2	F
1994 *	1	3	2	F
1995 *	1	3	2	F
1996 *	1	3	2	F
1997 *	1	3	2	F
1998 *	1	3	2	F
1999 *	1	3	2	F
2000 *	1	3	2	F
2001 *	1	3	2	F
2002 *	1	2	1.5	F
2003 *	1	2	1.5	F
2004 *	1	2	1.5	F
2005 *	1	2	1.5	F
2006 *	1	2	1.5	F
2007 *	1	2	1.5	F
2008 *	1	2	1.5	F

*: indicates electoral democracy

(Freedom House 2009a, b)

Table 2: Legislature Index of Electoral Competitiveness

Scale:	No legislature	1
	Unelected legislature	2
	Elected, 1 candidate	3
	1 party, multiple candidates	4
	Multiple parties are level but only one party won seats	5
	Multiple parties did win seats but the largest party received more than 75 percent of the seats	6
	Largest party got less than 75 percent	7

(Keefer et al. 2006)

Table 3: Executive Index of Electoral Competitiveness

Scale:	No executive	1
	Unelected executive	2
	Elected, 1 candidate	3
	1 party, multiple candidates	4
	Multiple parties are level but only one party won seats	5
	Multiple parties did win seats but the largest party received more than 75 percent of the seats	6
	Largest party got less than 75 percent	7

(Keefer el al. 2006)

Table 4: Legislature and Executive Index of Electoral Competitiveness of Greece, Period 1975 - 2006

Year	LIEC	EIEC
1975	7	7
1976	7	7
1977	7	7
1978	7	7
1979	7	7
1980	7	7
1981	7	7
1982	7	7
1983	7	7
1984	7	7
1985	7	7
1986	7	7
1987	7	7
1988	7	7
1989	7	7
1990	7	7
1991	7	7
1992	7	7
1993	7	7
1994	7	7
1995	7	7
1996	7	7
1997	7	7
1998	7	7
1999	7	7
2000	7	7
2001	7	7
2002	7	7
2003	7	7
2004	7	7
2005	7	7
2006	7	7

(World Bank 2009)

References

Beck , Thorsten et al (2001) New Tools in Comparative Political Economy: The Database of Political Economy, *The World Bank Economic Review* 15(1), 165-176.

Bogaards, Matthijs (2007) Elections, Election Outcomes and Democracy in Southern Africa, *Democratization* 14(1), 73-91.

Caramani, Daniele (2008) Party Systems, in Caramani (2008) *Comparative Politics*, 318-347.

Freedom House (2009a) Country ratings and status, FIW 1973-2009. *Freedom in the World Comparative and Historical Data*. Retrieved November 14, 2009: http://www.freedomhouse.org/uploads/fiw09/CompHistData/FIW_AllScores_Countries.xls

Freedom House (2009b) Electoral democracies, FIW 1989-90-2009. *Freedom in the World Comparative and Historical Data*. Retrieved November 14, 2009: http://www.freedomhouse.org/uploads/fiw09/CompHistData/ElectoralDemocracyTable.xls

Freedom House (2009c) Retrieved November 14, 2009: http://www.freedomhouse.org/template.cfm?page=15

Inter-Parliamentary Union (2009) Historical Archive of Parliamentary election results. *Greece.* Retrieved November 14, 2009: http://www.ipu.org/parline/reports/2125_arc.htm

Keefer, Philip et al. (2006) DPI 2006 Database Political Institutions: Changes and Variables Definitions. *Database of Political Institutions.* Retrieved November 14, 2009: http://siteresources.worldbank.org/INTRES/Resources/469232-1107449512766/dpi2006_vote_share_variable_definitions.pdf

Puddington, Arch (2009) The 2008 Freedom House Survey: A Third Year of Decline, *Journal of Democracy* 20(2), 93-107.

World Bank (2009) Database of Political Institutions 2006. *Database of Political Institutions.* Retrieved November 14, 2009: http://siteresources.worldbank.org/INTRES/Resources/469232-1107449512766/dpi2006_rev42008.xls